EXPOSING

The
MAP
REVOLUTION

AUTHOR OF *THE IDENTITY THEFT*
DOMINIQUAE
BIERMAN, PHD

Published by Zion's Gospel Press

52 Tuscan Way, Ste 202-412
St. Augustine, FL, 32092
shalom@zionsgospel.com

Paperback ISBN: 978-1-953502-51-3
E-Book ISBN: 978-1-953502-52-0

On occasion words such as Jesus, Christ, Lord and God have been changed by the author, back to their original Hebrew renderings, Yeshua, Messiah, Yahveh, and Elohim.

Bold or italicized emphasis or underlining within quotations is the author's own.

Printed in the United States of America

First Printing April 2006, Second Printing May 2020, Third Printing June 2021

Dedication

I dedicate this book with all my heart to all bishops, pastors, leaders, and ministers of the Body of Messiah. I hope and pray we will all be courageous enough to partake of the MAP Revolution and lead it ... for the sake of humanity and the glory of the Most High God!

Foreword

I chose the word *revolution* rather than reformation, transformation, or revival because the word *revolution* contains all of these. The End time MAP Movement is a *revolution*, and only when we see it as such will we be able to flow with it and with its Originator – the Almighty Himself! Just as the Jewish people are coming back from 2,000 years of exile, so is the Body of Yeshua coming back "home" to the Hebrew foundations of faith, after 1600 years of forced exile since the Council of Nicaea in the year 325.

For the End time revival—Archbishop Dr. Dominiquae Bierman Ph.D., President of *Kad-Esh MAP Ministries* and the *United Nations for Israel* in Jerusalem, Israel

CONTENTS

Part One

Restoring the Original Blueprint

*"For, if their rejection is the reconciliation of
the world, what will their acceptance be but life
from the dead?"*
—Romans 11:15

SINCE THE AZUZA STREET Revival in 1906, there is a variant that we have to reckon with if we are to see the next wave of Revival—Israel has come back to life. The Jewish people are again living in their own Promised Land after 2,000 years of painful exile, and Jerusalem is still its capital. There are more Jewish believers in Israel today than at any time in history apart from the first century. Any revival now will be contingent on how the international community of believers relate to Israel and all that Israel represents – a Holy people and the Holy Book.

"For, if their rejection is the reconciliation of the world, what will their acceptance be but life from the dead?" (Romans

11:15). The acceptance of the Jews and their restoration is *life* from the *dead* to the church and the world. That is *revival*!

Fly with me in your spirit to the Book of the Acts of the Apostles and to that period. Imagine that emerging congregation of Jewish disciples with their zeal, their passion, their devotion, and their holiness. Imagine them worshipping the Messiah with their hearts enraptured in His love, attentive to every word, and ready to fulfill every command, even martyrdom, if necessary. Imagine the anxious expectation of all the sick and oppressed in Jerusalem who from very early in the morning were waiting for Peter or one of the 12 to pass by, just so that their shadow could cover them and heal them. Imagine being so anointed and empowered by the Spirit, the Ruach ADONAI, that even your shadow would cause healing and transformation wherever you go! Imagine the faith and the boldness to speak the truth to their own people with no fear of men, being willing to be punished and beaten if needed. Imagine the *love* and the *urgency,* the *passion* that inspired them...

And now fly higher in your imagination and see the community of believers in Jerusalem, who were all Jewish believers at first. They knew the Holy Scriptures and knew the Commandments. Remember that the Fear of God in that community and the holiness and the purity were so great that a person found breaking the commandment of "you shall not lie" died in the presence of the Apostle because of breaking a financial vow. Anannias and Saphiras were carried out by the young men with no regrets as they had *offended the spirit of grace*!

Then Peter said to her, "Why is it that you have agreed together to put the Spirit of Yahveh to the test? Behold, the feet of those who have buried your husband are at the door, and they will carry you out as well." And immediately she fell at his feet and breathed her last, and the young men came in and found her dead, and they carried her out and buried her beside her husband. And great fear came over the whole church, and over all who heard of these things.

—Acts 5:9-11

Breaking the Father's Commandments brought *instant* death as it *tested the Holy Spirit*! The Holy Spirit was their guide, their "Torah Teacher" (instructor in the laws and ways of the Father). The Holy Spirit led them into *all truth*! Lies were not acceptable!

Imagine the awesome *love* that possessed that community where all shared together their finances and their possessions and all trusted the apostolic leadership to feed them both physically and spiritually. The Apostles distributed the funds as the Spirit of Holiness showed them, and *not one lacked*! Imagine the unity, the accountability, the submission to trusted authority. All that without compromising holiness and the Commandments of the Father just like Yeshua never compromised truth but rather walked in *truth* and *obedience* – He is *the truth*!

Let us continue our spiritual flight back to the First community of Jewish believers 2,000 years ago. Imagine the *awe*, the *signs*, the *wonders*, the *love*, the *holiness*, the *glory...* the *incredible unity between them all.* Jerusalem had never seen anything like this before! The Holy City was in *revival*, and new disciples were added to their numbers daily. The community of believers rejoiced as they broke bread from house to house, and those outside of the faith honored and feared them. They were impacting their Israeli society at all levels!

This was the original "church" or community of believers, and as with all "first things," They belong to Yahveh (the LORD). They also show us an example to follow and a pattern to imitate. This First community (or Early church as many call it) of believers was mostly if not entirely Jewish. Why is this so important? Because when we find the *blueprint* of a building, we can then proceed to *restore* it. The blueprint of the true church is based on the Holy Scriptures as revealed instructions on how to live for His glory on this earth.

Today the 21st century church is celebrating 100 years since the Azusa Street Revival, which changed the body of Messiah and transformed it in the power of the Holy Spirit. He has been freshly poured out over these last 100 years in order to *restore the original blueprint* so that the Father's House can be built; the nations can be saved; Israel can be restored, and Yeshua's Bride can be ready for His return.

For us to go into the *next* phase of *revival*, we need to remove *all* that has hindered the Holy Spirit's Work.

Since He came to lead us into all *truth*, we must embrace *truth* and reject all lies which are the product of the Father of Lies – Satan himself! Restoring the original blueprint is nothing short of a *revolution*. It will lead us to *overthrow* all the lies that we have inherited throughout 1,900 years of a deadly theology called replacement theology. This was established as *law* in the 4th century church through an Ecumenical Council, called the Council of Nicaea. The *fruit* of this council has been:

- The loss of the original blueprint – the Hebrew Holy Scriptures
- The quenching of the work of the Holy Spirit
- Anti-Semitism and hatred of Jews and anything labeled Jewish
- Lawlessness and lack of holiness in the community of believers

The next phase of Holy Spirit Revival will take us through *repentance*, which in Hebrew means to *turn* or to *return back to the original*. True repentance leads to *restoration*. Everything that quenches the Holy Spirit must be discarded. Our utmost desire needs to be embracing the Spirit of Truth and holiness *together* with all His outworking* and miraculous manifestations. We need *all of Him*!

Part Two

The Key for End time Revival

"I will ask the Father, and He will give you
another Helper, that He may be with you
forever; that is the Spirit of Truth, whom the
world cannot receive, because it does not see
Him or know Him, but you know Him because
He abides with you and will be in you."
—John 14:16,17

WHEN THE HELPER COMES, whom I will send to you from the Father, that is the Spirit of Truth who proceeds from the Father, He will testify about Me,"

—John 15:26

"But when He, the Spirit of Truth, comes, He will guide you into all the truth; for He will not speak on His own initiative, but whatever He hears, He will speak; and He will disclose to you what is to come. "He will glorify Me, for He will take of Mine and will disclose it to you. "All things that the Father has are Mine; therefore I said that He takes of Mine and will disclose it to you. "A little while, and you will no longer see Me; and again a little while, and you will see Me."

—John 16:13-16

By saying, "All things of the Father are mine and He (the Spirit) will show it unto you," Yeshua was actually saying that the Holy Spirit came to teach us the Commandments and the ways of the Father. In Hebrew, that is called the Torah or the instructions of God in righteousness. So a *major* work of the Holy Spirit is to interpret and teach us the Laws of God or, as many call them, "The Laws of Moses" and the *truth* about them and how they apply to us, the modern-day community of anointed believers in Messiah, both Jews and Gentiles.

That is why Anannias and Saphiras died instantly. Because they tested the Spirit of Truth and rejected the Father's Commandments. Just as with Adam of old, the breaking of Elohim's (the Creator's) commandment brought spiritual death, so now in the Messianic Dispensation of Glory, it brought *instant* death, not only spiritual but also physical.

Walking in the truth means walking in the Holy Spirit, for He is the Spirit of Truth! We cannot separate the miraculous manifestations of the Holy Spirit from the *truth* of the Word that He came to teach us. We must embrace all the Work of the Holy Spirit! Since the 1906 outbreak of the Azuza Street Revival in Los Angeles, California, the infilling and works and manifestations of the Holy Spirit have been embraced by millions of believers worldwide. In order to go on in the *revival* that began 100 years ago, we must now embrace the Holy Spirit as our *truth teacher*, our *Torah teacher*. We must be willing to tackle truth without fear and without breaking the love commandment. This is the challenge of the 21st century community of believers.

"But speaking the truth in love, we are to grow up in all aspects into Him who is the head, even Messiah"

—Ephesians 4:15

The *growth* of the Body is contingent on "speaking the truth in love." Without truth, there is no real growth and no real unity!

In John 17, when Yeshua prayed for unity between the Jewish and the coming Gentile believers, He gave us the key for that unity that will make the world believe in the Messiah.

"Sanctify them in the truth; Your word is truth."

—John 17:17

Truth sanctifies us! We must be willing to tackle truth together without defensiveness and without breaking the love commandment. It is the Holy Spirit Himself in our midst that is yearning to be embraced as the Spirit of Truth. He is eager to teach us the Father's Commandments!

"That is, the one whose coming is in accord with the activity of Satan, with all power and signs and false wonders, and with all the deception of wickedness for those who perish because they did not receive the love of the truth so as to be saved. For

this reason, God will send upon them a deluding influence so that they will believe what is false, in order that they all may be judged who did not believe the truth, but took pleasure in wickedness."

—2 Thessalonians 2:9-12

Notice that after 100 years of the aftermath of the Azuza Street Revival, Satan is threatened by an empowered church and is ready to counterattack with counterfeit miracles in order to *discredit* the true Move of the Holy Spirit. The only way to prevent this is by *loving the truth* that the Holy Spirit came to teach us. Our love for the Spirit of Truth will make us immune to Satan's Counterfeit Fire.

Since you have in obedience to the truth purified your souls for a sincere love of the brethren, fervently love one another from the heart, for you have been born again not of seed which is perishable but imperishable, that is, through the living and enduring word of God. For, "ALL FLESH IS LIKE GRASS, AND ALL ITS GLORY LIKE THE FLOWER OF GRASS. THE GRASS WITHERS, AND THE FLOWER FALLS OFF, BUT THE WORD OF YHVH ENDURES FOREVER." And this is the Word which was preached to you.

—1 Peter 1:22-25

One of the greatest women of God who ever lived, Katherine Kullman, used to plead with her audience,

"Please do not grieve the Holy Spirit, He is all I have."

As you read this book, I entreat you with the same words, *"Please do not grieve the Holy Spirit by rejecting the Spirit of Truth. He is all I have."*

Please pray with me: Precious Holy Spirit, Spirit of Holiness, and Spirit of Truth, anoint me as I read this book. I receive You in all Your fullness. Please lead me unto all truth, remove any spiritual blindness and any lies hidden inside of me. Sanctify me by the truth and thrust me into the End time Revival. In Yeshua's Name, Amen.

"Do not quench the Spirit's Fire"

—1 Thessalonians 5:19

Part Three

Revolution

FROM THE WEBSTER'S COLLEGIATE Dictionary

1. The action by a celestial body of going around in an orbit of elliptic course; also apparent move of such body around the earth.

2. The time taken by a celestial body to make a complete round in its orbit.

3. The completion of a course (the years that it takes a celestial body to complete a course around its orbit).

4. A progressive motion of a body around a center or axis so that any line of the body remains parallel to and returns to its initial position.

5. A sudden, radical and complete change.

6. A fundamental change in political organization; the overthrow or renunciation of one government

or ruler and the substitution of another by the governed.

7. Activity or movement designed to effect fundamental changes in the socioeconomic situation.

Restoration

1. Bringing back to a former position or condition.
2. Restoring to an unimpaired or improved condition.
3. A representation or a reconstruction of the original form.

The Map Movement is a revolution, and its purpose is restoration.

"Therefore repent and return, so that your sins may be wiped away, in order that times of refreshing may come from the presence of YHVH; and that He may send Yeshua, the Messiah appointed for you, whom heaven must receive until the period of restoration of all things about which God spoke by the mouth of His holy prophets from ancient time."

—Acts 3:19-21

In these verses, we can see that in order for the Messiah to return, we need to: *Repent* so that there will be *revival* so that *all things* can be *restored*. That is a *revolution*.

Repentance, Revival, & Restoration

That is a complete heavenly course that will bring all things to their initial position by exercising sudden and radical fundamental changes that will improve the condition of the body of Messiah until it is fully restored and ready to receive the King.

The One that is completing His orbit around His earth is none other than the Almighty, who is eager to send His Son Yeshua back.

The closer we are to the end of His time, the faster things will begin to change, and the more radical the changes will be in order to restore all the true foundations that He originated. Everything that is not aligned with the axis or the center (Yeshua being the center) will either become aligned or removed altogether.

Everything that has been governing His Body, but not by Him, will be overthrown, and His government, as at first, will be restored.

For some, this will sound scary, and they will try to stop it with all their power "in the name of "God" or "Christianity," and they will find themselves fighting against the Mighty One of Israel Himself. For others, this will be the fulfillment of all their dreams, though it will not happen without cost or suffering.

Part Four

Why M.A.P.?

WHEN I WAS IN Bible School during the year 1990, I asked the Father, 'what is the name of our ministry?' He answered me in perfect Hebrew: KAD-ESH, which means Vessel of Fire, and then He added the acronym MAP, which means:

Messianic Apostolic Prophetic

Many years later, I understood that though Kad-Esh is the name and function of our ministry (to be a conductor of YAH'S (God's) Revival Fire), MAP is the description of an entire *movement* and not only a ministry.

Kad-Esh MAP Ministries was born in 1990 in Dallas, Texas, at Christ for the Nations Bible College.

I was born again in Jerusalem in 1988, and the account of my miraculous salvation can be ordered from our website in the book called *"Yes!"* I had a personal encounter with Yeshua like Paul on the road to Damascus that changed my life, and just like Shaul-Paul, I asked Him, "What do you want me to do Adon (LORD)?"

His answer was: "I want to *send* you;" in other words, apostolic ministry.

My God is no respecter of persons or of man-made theologies, so the fact that many people would oppose the positioning of a woman in apostolic ministry and leadership did no deter Him in the least. He has never allowed me to excuse myself on any grounds, and when I have, I have suffered a painful reprimand from Heaven.

When He gave me the acronym MAP and its meaning, I felt numb. I had never heard anything like this before, and I was barely a two-year-old believer! Only now in the 21st century is this acronym becoming clear. It is about the restoration of all things. It is about the restoration of the original Hebrew foundations of faith in the Messianic Body. (By Messianic I mean, the anointed Body that belongs to the Messiah, both Jews and Gentiles). It is time for the original Gospel made in Zion to come out of Jerusalem again,

"The word which Isaiah the son of Amoz saw concerning Judah and Jerusalem. Now it will come about that in the last days, the mountain of the house of YHVH Will be established as the chief of the mountains, and will be raised above the hills, and all the nations will stream to it. And many peoples will come and say, "Come, let us go up to the mountain of YHVH, to the house of the God of Jacob; that He may teach

us concerning His ways and that we may walk in His paths."
For the law will go forth from Zion and the Word of YHVH
from Jerusalem. And He will judge between the nations, and
will render decisions for many peoples; and they will hammer
their swords into plough-shares and their spears into pruning
hooks. Nation will not lift up sword against nation, And
never again will they learn war."

—Isaiah 2:1-4

Part Five

Why Is a Revolution Needed?

LET US TAKE A look at some well known political revolutions.

The American Revolution

(From Wikipedia, the free encyclopedia)

The American Revolution was a revolution that ended two centuries of rule of the Thirteen Colonies by the British Empire and created the modern United States of America. The Revolutionary era was both exhilarating and disturbing–a time of progress for some, dislocation for others. The American Revolution is the series of ideas and changes that resulted in the revolution and ensuing political separation of thirteen colonies in North America from the British Empire and the creation of the United States of America with a new political system. The American War of Independence, which lasted from 1775 to 1783, was one part of the revolution, but the revolution by the Americans began before the first shot was fired at Lexington and Concord and continued after the British surrender at Yorktown. Years later, in 1818, John Adams wrote: "The Revolution was affected before the War commenced," and "The Revolution was in the minds and hearts of the people."

Historians usually agree that the revolutionary era began in 1763 as Britain defeated France in the French and Indian War, and the military threat to the colonies from France ended. The end of the period is usually marked by as Treaty of Paris in 1783. However, references to the "revolutionary era" sometimes stretched to 1789, when a new government under George Washington began operating.

Interpretations about the effect of the revolution vary. At one end of the spectrum is the older view that the American Revolution was not "revolutionary" at all, that it did not radically transform colonial society but simply replaced a distant government with a local one. The more recent view pioneered by historians such as Bernard Bailyn, Gordon Wood, and Edmund Morgan is that the American Revolution was a unique and radical event, based on a new ideology of "republicanism," which produced deep changes that had a profound impact on world history

The American Revolution was the first wave of the Atlantic Revolutions that would also take hold in the French Revolution, the Haitian Revolution, and the Latin American wars of liberation. Aftershocks would also be felt in Ireland in the 1798 rising, in the Polish-Lithuanian Commonwealth, and in the Netherlands.

The Revolution had a strong immediate impact in Great Britain, Ireland, the Netherlands, and France. Many British and Irish Whigs had been openly indulgent to the Patriots in America, and the Revolution was the first lesson in politics for many European radicals who would later take on active roles during the era of the French Revolution. Jefferson's Declaration had an immediate impact on the French

Declaration of the Rights of Man and the Citizen of 1789.

The American Revolution affected the rest of the world. The thinkers of the Enlightenment only wrote that common people had the right to overthrow unjust governments. The American Revolution was a case of practical success, which provided the rest of the world with a 'working model.'

The American Revolution set an example to the people in Europe and other parts of the world. It encouraged the people to realize they had rights independent of the sovereign; it promoted republicanism to overthrow monarchs. It incited people to fight for their rights, and it showed them that it was possible to win even against the world's foremost power, Great Britain.

Nowhere was the influence of the American Revolution more profound than in Latin America, where American writings and the model of colonies, which actually broke free and thrived decisively, shaped their struggle for independence. Historians of Latin America have identified many links to the U.S. model. See John Lynch, "The Origins of Spanish American Independence," in *Cambridge History of Latin America* Vol. 3 (1985), pp 45-46 (Wikipedia Contributors)

We can see that the revolutions that have changed this world were connected with rebellion against monarchic governments, tyrants and dictators, that oppressed the people and enslaved them. So, their purpose was to break free from them...

So it is with a Spiritual Revolution! Its main purpose is to rebel against the powers of darkness that have been ruling us as tyrants and dictators through demonically inspired laws and theologies. Though the word rebellion is generally a negative word, in this context, rebellion is needed. If we are to live the Life of the Kingdom, we must rebel against the rule of the god of this world and of all religious systems: Satan!

"Submit therefore to God. Resist the devil and he will flee from you."

—James 4:7

Part Six

Some Revolutionary Ideas

From that time, Yeshua began to preach and say, "Repent, for the kingdom of heaven is at hand."
—Matthew 4:17

YESHUA WAS A REVOLUTIONARY and a revolution all by Himself. He challenged and radically changed the religious thinking of His time. He stirred up change wherever He went and rebelled against the rule of darkness in the people. He healed the sick, cast out devils, and rebuked the religious hypocrites in leadership! He Himself said that He did not come to bring peace but a sword of division,

"For I came to SET A MAN AGAINST HIS FATHER, AND A DAUGHTER AGAINST HER MOTHER, AND A DAUGHTER-IN-LAW AGAINST HER MOTHER-IN-LAW; AND A MAN'S ENEMIES WILL BE THE MEMBERS OF HIS HOUSEHOLD. He who loves father or mother more than Me is not worthy of Me; and he who loves son or daughter more than Me is not worthy of Me. And he who does not take his cross and follow after Me is not worthy of Me. He who has found his life will lose it, and he who has lost his life for My sake will find it."

—Matthew 10:34-39

He never called us to a religious system, be it Christianity or Orthodox Judaism, but rather to the Kingdom and to obedience to His Father's Commandments.

From that time, Yeshua began to preach and say, "Repent, for the kingdom of heaven is at hand."

—Matthew 4:17

"Do not think that I came to abolish the Law or the Prophets; I did not come to abolish but to fulfill. For truly I say to you, until heaven and earth pass away, not the smallest letter or stroke shall pass from the Law until all is accomplished. "Whoever then annuls one of the least of these commandments, and teaches others to do the same, shall be called least in the kingdom of heaven; but whoever keeps and teaches them, he shall be called great in the kingdom of heaven. For I say to you that unless your righteousness surpasses that of the scribes and Pharisees, you will not enter the kingdom of heaven."

—Matthew 5:17-20

From the beginning, the Creator was expecting His Creation to obey His Commandments. That is why the preacher in Ecclesiastes says,

The conclusion, when all has been heard, is: fear God and keep His commandments, because this applies to every person. For God will bring every act to judgment, everything which is hidden, whether it is good or evil.

—Ecclesiastes 12:13,14

Obedience to the Father's Commandments is totally opposed to man-made religious systems that are founded on half-truths and on the misinterpretations of Scripture and the legalistic traditions of men. All religious systems are a by-product of Adam's ingesting the deathly fruit of the Tree of Knowledge of Good and Evil.

Then Yahveh God took the man and put him into the Garden of Eden to cultivate it and keep it. Yahveh God commanded the man, saying, "From any tree of the garden you may eat freely; but from the tree of the knowledge of good and evil you shall not eat, for in the day that you eat from it you will surely die."

—Genesis 2:15-17

Unbeknown to most, Satan's rule was established in the church legally in the year 325 AD, through an Ecclesiastical Council called the First Council of Nicaea.

Most all the church at that time (predominantly Gentiles) fell into his trap and have been partially or fully trapped in it and blinded by it until this day. Some people have felt the tyranny of it all and have begun to rebel against it, but others are still asleep because of its soporific, hypnotic influence. The Shofar Call has already sounded from Heaven...

THE MAP REVOLUTION is here to overthrow the tyranny of this Council that has cost the deaths of millions of Jews, millions of deceived Christians, and has doomed all nations to destruction. Follow me as I expose Satan's Master Plan to destroy the world through replacement theology and religion!

Part Seven

Replacement Theology Exposed

"Beware of the false prophets, who come to you in sheep's clothing, but inwardly are ravenous wolves. You will know them by their fruits. Grapes are not gathered from thorn bushes nor figs from thistles, are they? So every good tree bears good fruit, but the bad tree bears bad fruit. "A good tree cannot produce bad fruit, nor can a bad tree produce good fruit. Every tree that does not bear good fruit is cut down and thrown into the fire. So then, you will know them by their fruits.
—Matthew 7:15-20

As YOU READ THE following article, keep the *fruit* in mind and what Yeshua said about bad fruit. Remember what He was going to do with it!

The Error of Replacement Theology

(Adjusted from the original article published by "Bridges for Peace")

Perhaps you have heard of the term replacement theology.

However, if you look it up in a dictionary of Church history, you will not find it listed as a systematic study. Rather, it is a doctrinal teaching that originated in the early Church. It became the fertile soil from which Christian anti-Semitism grew and has infected the Church for nearly 1,900 years.

What Is Replacement theology?

Replacement theology was introduced to the Church shortly after Gentile leadership took over from Jewish leadership. What are its premises?

Israel (the Jewish people and the land) has been replaced by the Christian Church in the purposes of God, or, more precisely, the Church is the historic continuation of Israel to the exclusion of the former.

The Jewish people are now no longer a "chosen people." In fact, they are no different from any other group, such as the English, Spanish, or Africans.

Apart from repentance, the new birth, and incorporation into the Church, the Jewish people have no future, no hope, and no calling in the plan of God. The same is true for every other nation and group.

Since Pentecost of Acts 2, the term "Israel," as found in the Bible, now refers to the Church.

The promises, covenants, and blessings ascribed to Israel in the Bible have been taken away from the Jews and given to the Church, which has superseded them. However, the Jews are subject to the curses found in the Bible as a result of their rejection of Christ.

How Do Replacement theologians Argue their Case? They Say:

(Note: added rebuttal to each point.)

To be a son of Abraham is to have faith in Jesus Christ. For them, Galatians 3:29 shows that sonship to Abraham is seen only in spiritual, not national terms: "And if you be Christ's, then you are Abraham's seed, and heirs according to the promise."

Rebuttal: While this is a wonderful inclusive promise for Gentiles, this verse does not exclude the Jewish people from their original covenant, promise, and blessing as the natural seed of Abraham. This verse simply joins the Gentile Christians to what God has already started with Israel.

The promise of the land of Canaan to Abraham was only a "starter." The real Promised Land is the whole world. They use Romans 4:13 to claim it will be the Church that inherits the world, not Israel. "For the promise that he should be the heir of the world was not to Abraham, or to his seed, through the law, but through the righteousness of faith."

Rebuttal: Where does this verse exclude Abraham and His natural prodigy, the Jews? It simply says that, through the law, they would not inherit the world, but this would be acquired through faith. This is also true of the Church.

The nation of Israel was only the seed of the future Church, which would arise and incorporate people of all nations (Mal. 1:11): "For from the rising of the sun, even unto the going down of the same, My Name shall be great among the nations, and in every place, incense shall be offered to My Name, and a pure offering for My Name shall be great among the nations, says the Lord of Hosts."

Rebuttal: This is great and shows that the Jewish people and Israel fulfilled one of their callings to be "a light to the nations" so that God's Word has gone around the world. It does not suggest God's dealing with Israel was negated because His Name spread around the world.

Yeshua (Jesus) taught that the Jews would lose their spiritual privileges and be replaced by another people (Matt. 21:43): "Therefore I am saying to you, 'the kingdom of God will be taken from you, and given to a nation bringing forth the fruits of it.'"

Rebuttal: In this passage, Yeshua (Jesus) was talking about the Priests and Pharisees, who failed as leaders of the people. This passage is not talking about the Jewish people or nation of Israel.

A true Jew is anyone born of the Spirit, whether he is racially Gentile or Jewish (Rom. 2:28-29): "For he is not a Jew who is one outwardly; neither is that circumcision which is outward in the flesh; But he is a Jew who is one inwardly; and circumcision is that of the heart, in the spirit and not in the letter; whose praise is not of men, but of God."

Rebuttal: This argument does not support the notion that the Church replaced Israel. Rather, it simply reinforces what had been said throughout the Hebrew Scriptures [the Old Testament], and it certainly qualifies the spiritual qualifications for Jews or anyone who professes to be a follower of the God of Israel.

Paul shows that the Church is really the same "olive tree" as Israel was. Therefore, to distinguish between Israel and the Church is, strictly speaking, false. Indeed, people of Jewish origin need to be grafted back into the Church (Rom 11:17-23).

Rebuttal: This claim is the most outrageous because this passage clearly shows that we Gentiles are the "wild olive branches" who get our life from being grafted into the olive tree. The tree represents the covenants, promises, and hopes of Israel (Eph. 2:12), rooted in the Messiah and fed by the sap, which represents the Holy Spirit, giving life to the Jews (the "natural branches") and Gentiles alike. We Gentiles are told to remember that the olive tree holds us up and *not* to be arrogant or boast against the "natural branches" because they can be grafted in again. The olive tree is *not* the Church. We are simply grafted into God's plan, which preceded us by 2,000 years.

All the promises made to Israel in the Old Testament, unless they were historically fulfilled before the coming of Jesus Christ, are now the property of the Christian Church. These promises should not be interpreted literally or carnally but spiritually and symbolically. References to Israel, Jerusalem, Zion, and the Temple, when they are prophetic, really refer to the Church (II Cor. 1:20). "For all the promises of God in Him (Jesus) are Yea, and in Him, Amen, unto the glory of God by us." Therefore, they teach that the New Testament needs to be taught figuratively, not literally.

Rebuttal: Shortly, we will look at the fact that the New Testament references to Israel clearly pertain to Israel, not the Church. Therefore, no promise to Israel and the Jewish people in the Bible is figurative, nor can they be relegated to the Church alone. The promises and covenants are literal. Many of them are everlasting, and we Christians can participate in them as part of our rebirth but not to the exclusion of Israel. The New Testament speaks of the Church's relationship to Israel and her covenants as being "grafted in" (Rom. 11:17), "brought near" (Eph. 2:13), "Abraham's offspring (by faith)" (Rom. 4:16), and "partakers" (Rom. 15:27), *not* as usurpers of the covenant and a replacement for physical Israel. We Gentile Christians simply joined into what God had been doing in Israel. God did not break His covenant promises with Israel (Rom. 11:29).

How Did the Position of the Early Church Fathers Affect the Church?

Let us look at a brief history of the first four centuries of Christianity, which established a "legacy of hatred" towards the Jewish people, something that was against the clear teaching of the New Testament.

In the first century AD, the church was well-connected to its Jewish roots, and Yeshua did not intend for it to be any other way. After all, Jesus is Jewish, and the basis of His teaching is consistent with the Hebrew Scriptures. In Matthew 5:17-18, He states: "Do not think that I have come to abolish the Law or the Prophets; I have not come to abolish them but to fulfill them. I tell you the truth, until heaven and earth disappear, not the smallest letter, not the least stroke of a pen, will by any means disappear from the Law until everything is accomplished." Before the First Jewish Revolt in AD 66, Christianity was basically a sect of Judaism, as were the Pharisees, Sadducees, and Essenes.

The antagonism of the early Christians towards the Jews was reflected in the writings of the early Church Fathers. For example, Justin Martyr (c. AD 160), in speaking to a Jew, said: "The Scriptures are not yours, but ours." Irenaeus, Bishop of Lyon (c. AD 177), declared: "Jews are disinherited from the grace of God." Tertullian (AD 160-230), in his treatise, "Against the Jews," announced that God had rejected the Jews in favor of the Christians.

In the early 4th century, Eusebius wrote that the promises of the Hebrew Scriptures were for Christians and not the Jews, though the curses were for the Jews. He argued that the Church was the continuation of the Old Testament and thus superseded Judaism. The young Church declared itself to be the true Israel, or "Israel according to the Spirit," heir to the divine promises. They found it essential to discredit the "Israel according to the flesh" to prove that God had cast away His people and transferred His love to the Christians.

At the beginning of the 4th century, a monumental event occurred for the Church, which placed "The Church Triumphant" over "Vanquished Israel." In AD 306, Constantine became the first Christian Roman

Emperor. At first, he had a rather pluralistic view and accorded Jews the same religious rights as Christians. However, in AD 321, he made Christianity the official religion of the Empire to the exclusion of all other religions. This signaled the end of the persecution of Christians but the beginning of discrimination and persecution of the Jewish people.

Already at the Church Council in Elvira (Spain) in AD 305, declarations were made to keep Jews and Christians apart. This included ordering Christians not to share meals with Jews, not to marry Jews, not to use Jews to bless their fields, and not to observe the Jewish Sabbath.

Imperial Rome, in AD 313, issued the Edict of Milan, which granted favor to Christianity while outlawing synagogues. Then, in AD 315, another edict allowed the burning of Jews if they were convicted of breaking the laws. As Christianity was becoming the religion of the state, further laws were passed against the Jews:

- The ancient privileges granted to the Jews were withdrawn.

- Rabbinical jurisdiction was abolished or severely curtailed.

- Proselytizing of Judaism was prohibited and made punishable by death.

Jews were excluded from holding high office or military careers.

These and other restrictions were confirmed over and over again by various Church Councils for the next 1,000 years.

In AD 321, Constantine decreed all business should cease on "The honored day of the sun." By substituting Sunday for Saturday as the day for Christian worship, he further advanced the split. This Jewish Shabbat/Christian Sunday controversy also came up at the first real ecumenical Council of Nicaea (AD 325), which concluded Sunday to be the Christian day of rest, although it was debated for long after that. In AD 325, the Council of Nicaea divorced the Church completely from the Jews and anything Jewish. (Bridges for Peace)

The Council of Nicaea

From the letter of the Emperor (Constantine) to all those not present at the council (found in Eusebius, Vita Const., Lib III 18-20):

When the question relative to the sacred festival of Easter arose, it was universally thought that it would be convenient that all should keep the feast on one day; for what could be more beautiful and more desirable than to see this festival, through which we receive the hope of immortality, celebrated by all with one accord and in the same manner? It was declared to be particularly unworthy for this, the holiest of festivals to follow the customs (the calculation) of the Jews who had soiled their hands with the most fearful of crimes and whose minds were blinded. In rejecting their custom, we may transmit to our descendants the legitimate mode of celebrating Easter; which we have observed from the time of the Savior's passion according to the day of the week).

We ought not, therefore, to have anything in common with the Jew, for the Savior has shown us another way; our worship following a more legitimate and more convenient course (the order of the days of the week): And consequently in unanimously adopting this mode, we desire, dearest brethren to separate ourselves from the detestable company of the Jew. For it is truly shameful for us to hear them boast that without their direction, we could not keep this feast. How can they be in the right, they who, after the death of the Savior, have no longer been led by reason but by wild violence, as their delusion may urge them? They do not possess the truth in this Easter question, for in their blindness and repugnance to all improvements, they frequently celebrate two Passovers in the same year. We could not imitate those who are openly in error.

How, then, could we follow these Jews who are most certainly blinded by error? For to celebrate a Passover twice in one year is totally inadmissible.

But even if this were not so, it would still be your duty not to tarnish your soul by communication with such wicked people (the Jews). You should consider not only that the number of churches in these provinces make a majority, but also that it is right to demand what our reason approves, and that we should have nothing in common with the Jews. (Dr. Henry R. Percival's "The Nicaean and post Nicaean Fathers." Vol. XIV Grand Rapid: Erdmans pub. 1979, pgs. 54-55)

The Fruit of the Council of Nicaea

Overnight, Christianity was given the power of the Imperial State, and the emperors began to translate the concepts and claims of the Christian theologians against the Jews and Judaism into practice. Instead of the Church taking this opportunity to spread its gospel message in love, it truly became the Church Triumphant, ready to vanquish its foes. After 321, the writings of the Church Fathers changed in character. No longer was it on the defensive and apologetic, but aggressive and directing its venom at everyone "outside of the flock," in particular the Jewish people who could be found in almost every community and nation. During this period, we find more examples of anti-Jewish bias in Church literature written by church leaders:

Hilary of Poitiers (AD 291-371) wrote:

"Jews are a perverse people accursed by God forever."

Gregory of Nyssa (died AD 394), Bishop of Cappadocia wrote:

"The Jews are a brood of vipers, haters of goodness..."

* St. Jerome (AD 347-407) describes the Jews as:

"... serpents, wearing the image of Judas, their psalms and prayers are the braying of donkeys."

At the end of the 4th century, the Bishop of Antioch, John Chrysostom (Golden Tongued), the great orator, wrote a series of eight sermons against the Jews. He had seen Christians talking with Jewish people, taking oaths in front of the Ark, and some were keeping the Jewish feasts. He wanted this to stop. In an effort to bring his people back to what he called "The true faith," The Jews became the whipping boy for his sermon series. To quote him, "The synagogue is not only a brothel and a theater; it is also a den of robbers and a lodging for wild beasts. No Jew adores God... Jews are inveterate murderers, possessed by the devil, their debauchery and drunkenness gives them the manners of the pig. They kill and maim one another..."

One can easily see that a Judeo-Christian who wanted to hold on to his heritage, or a Gentile Christian who wanted to learn more about the parent faith of Christianity, would have found it extremely difficult under this pressure.

Chrysostom further sought to separate Christianity totally from Judaism. He wrote in his 4th Discourse, "I have said enough against those who say they are on our side, but are eager to follow the Jewish rites... it is against the Jews that I wish to draw up my battle... Jews are abandoned by God and for the crime of deicide, there is no expiation possible."

Chrysostom was known for his fiery preaching against what he saw as threats to his flock, including wealth, entertainment, privilege, and outward adornment. However, his preaching against the Jewish community, which he believed had a negative influence on Christians, is inexcusable and blatantly anti-Semitic in its content. Another unfortunate contribution Chrysostom made to Christian anti-Semitism was to hold the whole Jewish people culpable for the killing of Christ.

In the fifth century, the burning question was: If the Jews and Judaism were cursed by God, then how can you explain their existence?

Augustine tackled this issue in his "Sermon Against the Jews." He asserted that even though the Jews deserved the most severe punishment for having put Jesus to death, they have been kept alive by divine providence to serve, together with their Scriptures, as witnesses to the truth of Christianity.

Their existence was further justified by the service they rendered to the Christian truth, in attesting through their humiliation, to the triumph of the church over the Synagogue. They were to be a "witness people"—slaves and servants who should be humbled.

So, by the Middle Ages, the ideological arsenal of Christian anti-Semitism was completely established. This was further manifested in a variety of precedent-setting events within the church, such as Patriarch Cyril, Bishop of Alexandria, expelling the Jews and giving their property to a Christian mob. From a social standpoint, the deterioration of the Jewish position in society was only beginning its decline. During this early period, the virulent Judeo-phobia was primarily limited to the clergy.

The monarchs of the Holy Roman Empire thus regarded the Jews as serfs of the chamber (servi camerae), and utilized them as slave librarians to maintain Hebrew writings. They also utilized the services of Jews in another enterprise – usury, or money lending. The loaning of money was necessary to a growing economy. However, usury was considered to endanger the eternal salvation of the Christian and was thus forbidden. So, the church endorsed the practice of lending by Jews, for according to their reasoning, their Jewish souls were lost in any case. Much later, the Jewish people were utilized by the Western countries as trade agents in commerce, and thus we see how the Jewish people found their way into the fields of banking and commerce.

The result of these anti-Jewish teachings continued onwards throughout church history, manifesting in such events and actions as the Crusades, the accusation of communion host desecration and blood libel by the Jews, the forced wearing of distinguishing marks to ostracize them, the Inquisition, the displacement of whole Jewish communities by exile or separate ghettoes, the destruction of synagogues and Jewish books, physical persecution and execution, and the Pogroms. Ultimately, the seeds of destruction grew to epic proportions, culminating in the Holocaust, which occurred in

"Christian" Europe. Protestant and Evangelical Christianity has been further infected with replacement theology and anti-Semitism through Martin Luther.

Martin Luther

Although Luther did not invent anti-Jewishness, he promoted it to a level never before seen in Europe. Luther bore the influence of his upbringing from anti-Jewish theologians such as Lyra, Burgensis (and John Chrysostom, before them). But Luther's 1543 book "On the Jews and their Lies" took Jewish hatred to a new level when he proposed to set fire to their synagogues and schools, to take away their homes, forbade them to pray or teach, or even to utter God's name. Luther wanted to "be rid of them" and requested that the government and ministers deal with the problem. He requested pastors and preachers to follow his example of issuing warnings against the Jews. He goes so far as to claim that, "We are at fault in not slaying them" for avenging the death of Jesus Christ. Hitler's Nazi government in the 1930s and 40s fit Luther's desires to a tee.

Martin Luther 'On the Jews & their Lies' Chapter 15

The following is an excerpt from Martin Luther's book "On the Jews and their lies." Adolph Hitler quoted Luther in his book "Mein Kampf" as an inspiration for his insatiable quest for the extermination of the Jewish people!

Excerpts

What shall we Christians do with this rejected and condemned people, the Jews? Since they live among us, we dare not tolerate their conduct. With prayer and the fear of God, we must practice a sharp mercy to see whether we might save at least a few from the glowing flames. We dare not avenge ourselves. Vengeance a thousand times worse than we could wish them already has them by the throat. I shall give you my sincere advice:

First, to set fire to their synagogues or schools and to bury and cover with dirt whatever will not burn, so that no man will ever again see a stone or cinder of them. This is to be done in honor of our Lord and of Christendom, so that God might see that we are Christians,

Second, I advise that their houses also be razed and destroyed. For they pursue in them the same aims as in their synagogues. Instead they might be lodged under a roof or in a barn, like the gypsies. This will bring home to them the fact that they are not masters in our country, as they boast, but that they are living in exile and in captivity, as they incessantly wail and lament about us before God.

Third, I advise that all their prayer books and Talmudic writings, in which such idolatry, lies, cursing, and blasphemy are taught, be taken from them.

Fourth, I advise that their rabbis be forbidden to teach henceforth on pain of loss of life and limb.

Fifth, I advise that safe-conduct on the highways be abolished completely for the Jews. For they have no business in the countryside, since they are not lords, officials, tradesmen, or the like. Let them stay at home.

Sixth, I advise that usury be prohibited to them, and that all cash and treasure of silver and gold be taken from them and put aside for safekeeping. Moreover, since priesthood, worship, government with which the greater part, indeed, almost all, of those laws of Moses deal have been at an end for over fourteen hundred years already, it is certain that Moses' law also came to an end and lost its authority. Therefore the imperial laws must be applied to these imperial Jews. Their wish to be Mosaic Jews must not be indulged. In fact, no Jew has been that for over fourteen hundred years.

Seventh, I recommend putting a flail, an axe, a hoe, a spade, a distaff, or a spindle into the hands of young, strong Jews and Jewesses and letting them earn their bread in the sweat of their brow, as was imposed on the children of Adam (Gen. 3 [:19]).

In brief, dear princes and lords, those of you who have Jews under your rule: if my counsel does not please you, find better advice, so that you and we all can be rid of the unbearable, devilish burden of the Jews. (Martin Luther, *On the Jews and their Lies*, chapter 15)

Luther & Hitler

In *Mein Kampf*, Hitler listed Martin Luther as one of the greatest reformers. And similar to Luther in the 1500s, Hitler spoke against the Jews. The Nazi plan to create a German Reich Church laid its basis on the "Spirit of Dr. Martin Luther." The first physical violence against the Jews came on November 9-10 on *Kristallnacht* (Crystal Night) when the Nazis killed Jews, shattered glass windows, and destroyed hundreds of synagogues, just as Luther had proposed. In Daniel Johah Goldhagen's book, *Hitler's Willing Executioners*, he writes:

> "One leading Protestant churchman, Bishop Martin Sasse, published a compendium of Martin Luther's anti-Semitic vitriol shortly after *Kristallnacht's* orgy of anti-Jewish violence. In the foreword to the volume, he applauded the burning of the synagogues and the coincidence of the day: 'On November 10, 1938, on Luther's birthday, the synagogues are burning in Germany.' the German people, he urged, ought to heed these words 'of the greatest anti-Semite of his time, the warner of his people against the Jews.'" (Jim Walker, *Hitler's Willing Executioners*)

The Fruit of Luther's Writings?

Six million Jews exterminated during the Holocaust in Nazi Europe, choked to death in gas chambers, and burned in ovens. And all Christendom stood silent, let it happen, and even cooperated.

Nowadays, most of Christianity is silent or cooperating with the establishing of a Palestinian Terror State in the Land of Israel. There is a plan to exterminate the Jews again.

Where is the Church?

Had the Church understood the clear message of being grafted into the Olive Tree from the beginning, then the sad legacy of anti-Semitic hatred from the Church may have been avoided. The error of replacement theology is like a cancer in the Church that has not only caused it to violate God's Word concerning the Jewish people and Israel, but it made us into instruments of hate, not love in God's Name.

The Jews Are Still Chosen

The clear teaching of the New Testament is that the Church was and is to love and honor the Jewish people. In Ephesians 2:11-18, we are told that *"by the blood of Messiah"* we Gentiles are *"made near"* to the commonwealth of Israel, the covenants, promises, and hopes given to Israel. In Romans 11:11-12, 25, we are told that *"blindness in part"* has come to the Jews so that the message would be forced out into the nations. Nevertheless, we are told that a time would come when *"all Israel would be saved*" (v. 26) because the gifts and callings of God towards Israel and the Jewish people were given without repentance (v. 29). God's relationship with Israel and the Jewish people is everlasting. We Gentile Christians are told that the Jews are *"beloved for the sake of the Patriarchs"* (Rom. 11:28). They are a chosen people who fulfilled their calling and brought the gospel to the world. They were chosen to:

Be obedient to God's Word and to be as "a light to the nations."

- Hear God's Word and record it – the Bible.
- Be the human channel for the Messiah.

Thanks to the Jews, We Have the Bible

The Jewish people have fulfilled their role. The promise to the world through Abraham was that, *"in you will all the nations on the earth be blessed"* (Gen. 12:3). They were to be a light unto the nations and, while they made mistakes as we all do, they did demonstrate the power of God on earth. They did hear God's Word and record it so that we have the Bible, and they were the human channel for the Messiah. He was born, ministered, died, rose from the dead, ascended to heaven and will return to Jerusalem, Israel, in a day yet to come.

An Everlasting Covenant

God made an everlasting covenant between the land of Israel and the Jewish people that must be fulfilled and completed, or His Word - the Bible, would be proven a lie - which it is not. God will never forget or annul His covenant with His ancient people. If God will not fulfil His promises to Israel, what guarantee do we have that He will fulfil His promises to the Church? (See Jeremiah 31:35-37).

According to Romans 11, we are two distinct groups, both grafted into the same tree, which is comprised of the covenants and promises given to Israel. We are grounded into the same root, the Messiah; drinking of the same sap, God's Holy Spirit. We do not hold up the tree, but the tree us, and we are forbidden from boasting against or being arrogant towards God's covenant people the Jews (Rom. 11:17-18).

What Happens When the Church *Replaces* Israel?

- the church becomes arrogant and self-centred.
- It boasts against the Jews and Israel.
- It devalues the role of Israel or has no role for Israel at all.

These attitudes result in anti-Semitism in word and deed.

Without a place for Israel and the Jewish people today, you cannot explain the Bible prophecies, especially the very specific ones being fulfilled in Israel today.

Many New Testament passages do not make sense when the Jewish people are replaced by the church.

You can lose the significance of the Hebrew Scriptures, the Old Testament, for today. Many Christians boast of being a New Testament (NT) Christian or a NT church as in the Book of Acts. However, the Bible of the early church was not the New Testament, which did not get codified until the 4th century, but rather the Hebrew Scriptures.

You can lose the Hebraic/Judaic contextualization of the New Testament, which teaches us more about Yeshua and how to become better disciples.

The church loses out on the opportunity to participate in God's plan. Endless divisions and denominations in the church.

What Happens When the Church *Relates* & Is Grafted Into Israel?

- the church loves, honors, and blesses Israel and is blessed in return. Genesis 12:3.
- The church walks in holiness and righteousness, having God's laws and commandments written in our hearts. Jeremiah 31:31-33
- The nations are saved. Matthew 25:32
- The Jewish people can recognize their Messiah.

We value the Old and New Testaments as equally inspired and significant for the Church today.

Bible prophecy makes sense for today and offers opportunities for involvement in God's plan for Israel.

We become better disciples of Yeshua (Jesus) as we are able to appreciate the Hebraic/Judaic roots that fill in the definitions, concepts, words, and events in the New Testament that are otherwise obscured. Why? Many were not explained by the Jewish writers of the New Testament because they did not feel the need to fill in all the details that were already explained in the Old Testament.

Had the church understood this very clear message from the beginning, then the sad legacy of anti-Semitic hatred from the church may have been avoided. The error of replacement theology is like a cancer in the church that has not only caused it to violate God's Word concerning the Jewish people and Israel, but it made us into instruments of hate, not love, in God's Name. Yet, it is not too late to change our ways and rightly relate to the Jewish people and Israel today.

Fruit of Replacement Theology at a Glance

- Divorce from the original Jewish foundations and from the Jewish Messiah
- Hatred and murder of millions in the name of Christ (mainly of Jews)
- Mixture of paganism and Babylonian worship (Sunday, Christmas, Easter)
- The establishing of a religious Christian system rather than the advancing of the Kingdom
- Loss of the true Gospel of the Kingdom
- Lack of fear of God
- Lack of holiness and Power
- Healing and miracles ceased
- It thrust the church into the Dark Ages
- Loss of honor and obedience to God's Commandments

An urgent solution must be applied; prior to the return of Messiah, we must be sanctified from *replacement theology, all its hatred, mixture, and unrighteousness. We must become a Bride pure and holy calling a lost world back to the holy God of Israel*

Our Radical Priority

- Seek to walk in burning love and obedience to the Father's Commandments.
- To bring His love to Israel and the true Gospel of the Kingdom to all nations, followed with demonstrations of His healing, deliverance, and miracle-working power and His passion and compassion for lost humanity; to the Jew first and also to the Gentile.

All of our lives need to be submitted to this one cause: Seek to advance His Kingdom through *everything* He calls us to do!

"Then Yeshua said to his disciples, "If any man desires to come after me, let him deny himself, and take up his cross, and follow me. For whoever desires to save his life will lose it, and whoever will lose his life for my sake will find it. For what will it profit a man, if he will gain the whole world, and forfeit his life? Or what will a man give in exchange for his life? For the Son of Man will come in the glory of his Father with his angels, and then will he render to every man according to his deeds."

—Matthew 16:24-27

Time to Repent[*]

"So, because you are lukewarm, and neither hot nor cold, I will vomit you out of my mouth."

—Revelation 3:16

"Not everyone who says to me, 'LORD, LORD,' will enter into the Kingdom of Heaven; but he who does the will of my Father who is in heaven."

—Matthew 7:21

The Fruit of the Nations Pushing Israel for False Peace With Terrorists (See Psalms 83 on the subject)

An Important Prayer

Dear Father in Heaven, I come before you in all humility to ask your forgiveness for my ignorant involvement in replacement theology in any of its aspects. I totally renounce replacement theology, the Council of Nicaea, and Babylonian Christianity. I break the hold of any spirit connected with it over my life and faith. I accept you, Yeshua, as my Jewish Messiah and commit myself to love your Jewish people and your Holy Commandments. Thank you for your

---

[*] See at the end of this book Revocation of the Council of Nicaea

great mercy and for granting me a fresh start as an enlisted soldier in this End time Spiritual revolution. Here I am ADONAI (LORD). Use me to bring life where Christianity has brought death and especially to the Jewish people. In Yeshua's Name. Amen.

Part Eight

The Fruit of Religion
– No Sheep Nations

"All the nations will be gathered before Him,
and He will separate them one from another,
as a shepherd divides his sheep from his goats.
And He will set the sheep on his right hand,
but the goats on the left."
—Matthew 25:32

THE FOLLOWING IS AN excerpt of my book "Sheep Nations."

A Visitation in Chile, Argentina 2001

In late December 2001, Baruch and I personally witnessed the Argentinean Uprising. It seemed as though the whole nation had spilled over onto the streets, protesting the government and the banking system. Hard-working people had deposited their money in the banks, but when they needed to withdraw it, the banks had no money to give them. Much of the nation was left cashless and penniless, and the hearts were boiling. This was a nation in bankruptcy!

We had landed in Argentina only twenty-four hours before this fateful day. As is our custom, whenever we arrive in any nation to which we are sent, we blow the shofar at the airport, "The gate" of the nation, or both. Argentina was no exception. Twenty-four hours later, this mass protest exploded. A sea of people of all ages: The young, old, and babies; fathers and mothers with their children all flooded the main streets of Buenos Aires headed to the Presidential Palace – *La Casa Rosada*, or the Pink House. Our hotel was within walking distance from La Casa Rosada, and we witnessed this event right before our eyes. We decided to take our video camera to act as 'prophetic journalists' and ventured out into this wave of anger, frustration, and solidarity of the Argentinean people. Of course, the hotel staff warned us of the danger of getting ourselves killed in the midst of the mob, but we informed them that we had a special Angelic Escort. With that, we ventured out to an amazing experience.

Later on, the radio reported that several were injured and that most of the supermarkets were being looted by either hungry people, angry people, or both. We also witnessed when the Presidential helicopter took off from the roof of La Casa Rosada with the president fleeing Argentina. The people had managed to run the president off!

Meanwhile, we were literally trapped in our hotel. All of our meetings for that day had to be canceled, including a pastor's meeting. One dear friend, a pastor, and host, asked me half-jokingly in Spanish, my mother tongue, "Dominiquae what on earth did you do when you arrived in Argentina?" to which I replied, "Nothing, I just blew the shofar at the airport of Eseiza."

(This was not, nor would be, the only serious occurrence following my blowing the shofar, the silver trumpet, or both in a nation or a region.)

"Over a million intercessors have been praying for a change of government in Argentina," he added. It was then I connected why Yeshua told me to come to Argentina at this time.

A few weeks earlier, I had called a very good friend of mine, a great lover of Israel, Evangelist Alberto Mottessi, and told him that Yah was sending me to Argentina. He wanted to organize some big meetings there, but I said that my time was short and that I needed to be there in two weeks, which would not give him sufficient time to organize much. Nevertheless, many wonderful pastor friends such as Julio Donati received me well and blessed us. And, God had organized a greater meeting than anyone could have put together – a massive demonstration of all the people of Argentina in every major city and town. We got to blow the shofar before it began, be witnesses while it was going on, and walk the streets of the capital after it had subsided. This is what we saw on the day after the uprising:

Walking on the street that leads to La Casa Rosada, we saw many buildings damaged by stones or bullet holes. There were burnt tires strewn here and there, and nearly every building had walls or windows damaged. One particular building caught our attention because it had been damaged far more than any other. This building was riddled with bullet holes, and all of its glass completely smashed. It was an imposing building with very dark glass, and it seemed that the mob was particularly angry with this building. As we were observing the damage and pondering as to the 'why' of this, I noticed police cars next to this building, and then I read the address. I remembered that address: This was none other than the Israeli Embassy of Buenos Aires!

Why would the mob take revenge against the Israeli Embassy for Argentina's financial distress? It immediately brought to mind Nazi Germany in 1933 when Hitler came into power and made the Jews the 'scapegoat' for all of Germany's financial problems. After all the events from 1933 through 1945, as well as the occurrences of the terrible Second World War, including the atrocious Holocaust, which left us Jews bereaved of more than six million. It was clear to me that nothing had changed. The nations were still full of hatred towards the Jews. Given the 'right' kind of circumstances, the Jews would be blamed and persecuted again. It did not surprise us when we received the report that the Jewish Agency was organizing a massive *Aliyah,* immigration to Israel, of Jews from Argentina, *one* day after the mass uprising took place in

December of 2001. Since then, many, but not enough, Jews have come home to Israel from Argentina.

Chile 2001

Baruch and I arrived in my native land of Chile on December 24th, 2001, and nestled ourselves in a hotel in Santiago. We were to minister two days later in Valparaiso near the seaport, plus I was greatly anticipating a reunion with many of my relatives, especially my elderly maternal grandmother.

The 25th of December came, and I rose to pray quite early. However, I ventured out onto the balcony of my room to pray in privacy. What happened next completely caught me off guard. I have had many visitations from the LORD, both dreams and open visions, but I've never heard the LORD so clearly asking me such a serious question before. When ADONAI asks a question, it is not because He does not know the answer! So I knew that He was trying to impart to me a message that I know now has become the major thrust of our ministry.

Preparing to pray, I settled comfortably in a chair, looking out from the balcony. The presence of *Yah* absorbed me, and I do not even remember the view from that balcony, uncharacteristic of me who never forgets a view! I only remember His question. It resonated into my entire being:

"Dominiquae, what would happen if I came back right *now*? How many nations would be Sheep Nations?"

"You see," He said, "I will judge the nations by these two standards:

- My Eternal, *Unchanging* Righteous Law
- By how the nations treat *My* Jewish people

He had my attention! Rapidly, passages of Scripture ran through my mind. One was Matthew 25:32: He will gather the nations and will separate them as the sheep from the goats. I considered many other verses. It did not take but a second for me to say, "*None LORD.*"

As He was talking, my spirit, mind, and heart were racing at the speed of light. It was like the whole Bible was opening before me with a new understanding and clarity about the condition of the world and of the nations, one like I had never had before! This was a Visitation from *Yah,* the Almighty was manifesting His will to His soldier, and I was listening.

"I gave My disciples the commission to disciple the nations, all the ethnic groups of the earth, and to teach them My Commandments. I said to make disciples of all nations, and yet after 2,000 years of My gospel being on earth, you cannot present to Me one Sheep Nation!"

I knew that He was right. Not one nation had adopted Yahveh's commandments as their constitution. Neither was there any nation that I knew of that was guiltless concerning Israel. In 1938, a time when Hitler had already begun His plan to rid the world of its Jews, an international convention met in Evian, France, to discuss the "Jewish Problem." Not one nation was willing to give shelter to even some of the Jews from Germany and Europe in order to rescue them from Hitler's claws (except the Dominican Republic, who was willing to take a few of those who knew agriculture).

"For I was hungry, and you gave Me no food; I was thirsty, and you gave Me no drink; I was a stranger, and you did not take Me in, naked and you did not clothe Me, sick and in prison (in concentration camps and ghettos!), and you did not visit Me...Assuredly I say to you, inasmuch as you did not do it to the least of these you did not do it to Me."

—Matthew 25:42-45

All nations knew what was happening. U.S. bombers flew over Auschwitz countless times. They could have bombed the death camps of Birkenau but did not. England knew. The church knew, but not one denomination arose to oppose Hitler or the Holocaust.

We took a tour to Auschwitz in March 2003 and were shocked by a new exhibition on display. This exhibition consisted of documents and pictures detailing how the church of its time, both Catholic and Protestant, had given Hitler their blessing as he entered into government. Later on, not one church group or organization stood up to oppose him!

Here and there, individuals such as Corrie Ten Boom and Oscar Schindler stood bravely for what was right, but by far, they were the minority. They were not part of any church or national effort; they were acting on their own.

I was beginning to get the picture. If Yeshua returned that day (Christmas Day 2001) *all* the nations, including the USA, Switzerland, Australia, Italy, Chile, Argentina, et cetera, would be judged as goat nations.

"Then He will say to those in the left hand, 'Depart from Me you cursed, into the everlasting fire prepared for the devil and his angels.'"

—Matthew 25:41

In other words, all the nations of the earth are under a curse!

"I will bless those who bless you, and I will curse him who curses you; and in you, all the families of the earth will be blessed (*if* they bless you!)"

—Genesis 12:3

More Scriptures began to come to mind as the Holy Spirit, the Ruach HaKodesh, was leading me into the understanding of Yahveh's message. He took me to Isaiah 34:1-8.

"Come near, you nations, to hear; and heed you people! Let the earth hear. And all that is in it, the world and all things that come forth from it."

—Isaiah 34:1

I was 'earth,' and I was listening!

"For the indignation of the LORD is against all nations, and his fury against all their armies; He has utterly destroyed them, He has given them over to the slaughter."

—Isaiah 34:2

This is in past tense, which means that Yahveh has already done it in His mind. It is a 'done deal' and ready to be manifested in the natural.

There are no speculations here; the LORD has already decided to destroy all the nations, not one Sheep Nation in sight!

"Also, their slain shall be thrown out, their stench shall rise from their corpses, and the mountains shall be melted with their blood. All the host of heaven shall be dissolved...For it is the day of the LORD's vengeance, the year of recompense for the cause of Zion."

—Isaiah 34: 3-4, 8

Yahveh has spoken, and Yahveh will do it.

I was trembling before the LORD as He kept on speaking to me:

"Dominiquae, the devil has always wanted to destroy Israel, and through Israel, also to cause Me to judge all the nations. Satan's desire is not only to annihilate Israel but the whole human race. His plan has been to cause people to hate My Torah, My righteous laws, and My people, the Jews. I called the Ekklesia, My called-out ones, to teach the nations to love My Holy Commandments and to love all peoples, especially the Jews, My chosen ones."

I broke before My Father, the Judge of the Universe who is love, and said:

"Father, we the church have failed to teach the nations and to make disciples of all nations. After 2,000 years of 'gospel,' we have miserably failed the Great Commission. We, the church, have not done the job."

"The church has done the job," The LORD said to me in a very firm tone, "but she has done the job wrongly. The church

75

has used her authority to teach the nations to hate My Law and to hate My Jews."

My mind was spinning and my heart racing. Truly, historically speaking, every horrendous massacre of Jews from the second century and on has been carried out by the church, in the name of Christ, and due to anti-Semitic Christian doctrine. No one can refute, without making a fool of himself, that for the last 1,800 years, particularly the last 1,600 years since the infamous 'Council of Nicaea,' the Christian church has been the worst persecutor the Jewish people have ever known.

I have always felt surprised and distressed that Bible schools and seminaries do not teach this 'bloody history.' All the 'church History' books completely ignore the persecution of the Jews, which has been one of the most prevalent marks of the Christian Religion since it was officially instituted by Emperor Constantine and the Gentile church fathers in 325 A.D. Christian events such as the Spanish Inquisition, the Pogroms, the Crusades and the Holocaust are not studied in any Christian Bible school. If they are mentioned at all, they are treated lightly and quickly.

But it was on that Christmas Day of 2001 that the LORD visited me in Chile, one of the most anti-Semitic nations in the world; a country where *"The Holy Office,"* The institution of the Spanish Inquisition, still exists. It's a country that has given shelter to many officers of the Nazi Regime who are in hiding. It was there that the Almighty was visiting me and literally told me that the whole world was going to hell! And that the wrong teachings of the Christian church were sending them there!

He did not say, "Go into all the world and teach Christianity to the Nations. Turn them into pagans and teach them how to celebrate the false deities Tammuz and Ishtar during the foreign celebrations of Christmas and Easter." He did not say, "Go to the nations and tell them that My laws are done away with and that they are free from My laws." He did not tell them, "Go into all the nations and tell them that the Jews killed Christ, so they deserve to be second class citizens and live in hell forever as the Gentile church fathers, including John Chrisostom and St. Augustine, had told them." And He did not tell them to, "Go and tell the nations to get rid of the Jews because they are 'vermin' and a 'plague,' such as their father Martin Luther had told them..."

No, no, no! The Great Commission was given to His Jewish apostles, who were not Christian and knew nothing about Christianity. They were His disciples, His followers, and He had taught them Torah. They had celebrated the biblical Holy Days with Him. They had eaten 'Kosher' and clean food with Him. This is what He purposefully told His Jewish Disciples: "

All authority has been given unto Me in heaven and on earth. Go therefore and make disciples of all nations. Teaching them to observe (to do!) all things that I have commanded you; and lo, I am with you always and even to the end of the age."
—Matthew 28:18-20

I wept before the God of Heaven, Elohim the Creator, and began to repent on behalf of the church.

"LORD *forgive us!* Please give us more time that we might teach the nations Your Commandments and Your love for Israel."

I borrowed time from the God of Israel on that Christmas Day of 2001 in my native land of Chile. And since then, my dear people, we are running on borrowed time.

In my book, *The Healing Power of the Roots*, first printed in 1996, I said that the LORD had told me,

> Teaching the Jewish roots to the church was a matter of life and death as: The church had been like a beautiful rose cut off from her garden (Israel, the Jews, and the Torah) and put in a vase for two days. But if it's not replanted back in the original garden, on the third day, it will die. (Dominiquae Bierman, *The Healing Power of the Roots*)

Since I wrote that book, we have already entered into the Third Day, the Third Millennium...

And now Yahveh has visited me about the nations.

Preaching the Good News of Yeshua, the Jewish Messiah, teaching Yahveh's Torah, and teaching the nations to love Him and His Jewish people is a matter of life and death *to all* the nations of the earth!

"And it shall happen in that day that I will make Jerusalem a very heavy stone for all peoples; all who would heave it away will surely be cut in pieces, though all nations of the earth are gathered against it... It shall be on that day that I will seek to destroy all nations that come against Jerusalem."

—Zecharaiah 12:3,12

"Close your eyes for a moment and feel the pulsating rhythm of the 'Hate-the-Jew' song as it captivates the nations of the world. The Muslims are dancing to its beat. Communist China is familiar with its tune. Europe often moves to its tempo. Some Americans are humming along. The 'Church' has written the lyrics. And Satan is orchestrating it all!" (Michael L. Brown, *Our Hands are Stained with Blood,* page 162)

This information in itself should make us shudder. What kind of power is hiding behind replacement theology and religion that it has overpowered all nations and blinded them all to the true Gospel of the Kingdom? What dark, wicked power is operating behind it?

The following pictures are a reminder of this wicked power and its devastating effects on mankind. The Holocaust, or its real name "The Shoa," which means Total Devastation, is a *fruit* of the infamous replacement theology and Christianity as a religion. (Don't get upset with me before time! As you continue reading, I will prove this to you.)

Part Nine

Uprooting the Tree of Death

"Pursue peace with all men and holiness
without which no one will see the Lord Yeshua"
—Hebrews 12:14

Many times I have said that the Body of Yeshua needs to be grafted into the Olive Tree (Romans 11) and not the Christmas Tree, which is a pagan tradition.

Hear the word, which Yahveh speaks to you, O house of Israel. Thus says Yahveh, "Do not learn the way of the nations, And do not be terrified by the signs of the heavens Although the nations are terrified by them; For the customs of the peoples are delusion; Because it is wood cut from the forest, the work of the hands of a craftsman with a cutting tool.

— Jeremiah 10:1-3

The Tree of Christianity that grew out of the seeds of replacement theology needs to be uprooted altogether from the body of Messiah, from our mindsets, traditions, and doctrines. We cannot leave any trace of it lest it grows again and kills us. Many theology books which are taught in well-reputed Bible Seminaries are infested with replacement theology and need to be discarded lest they continue poisoning a new generation! We have no time to waste! Judgment has already begun in the House of the LORD!

"For it is time for judgment to begin with the household of God; and if it begins with us first, what will be the outcome for those who do not obey the gospel of God? AND IF IT IS WITH DIFFICULTY THAT THE RIGHTEOUS IS SAVED, WHAT WILL BECOME OF THE GODLESS MAN AND THE SINNER? Therefore, those also who suffer according to the will of God shall entrust their souls to a faithful Creator in doing what is right.

—Peter 4:17-19.

Everything that was changed and established during the Council of Nicaea needs to be reversed to the original, including God's Holy Shabbat as the weekly Holy Day and His Holy feasts and Convocations rather than the pagan feasts which have become the heritage of Christianity. It is now high time to restore the original blueprint! I am not talking about being "under the law" but rather *one* with the Law and the Lawgiver – Yeshua, the Jewish Messiah. That is why Yeshua said:

"Do not think that I came to abolish the Law or the Prophets; I did not come to abolish but to fulfill. For truly I say to you, until heaven and earth pass away, not the smallest letter or stroke shall pass from the Law until all is accomplished. Whoever then annuls one of the least of these commandments, and teaches others to do the same, shall be called least in the kingdom of heaven; but whoever keeps and teaches them, he shall be called great in the kingdom of heaven. For I say to you that unless your righteousness surpasses that of the scribes and Pharisees, you will not enter the kingdom of heaven."

—Matthew 5:17-20

He was saying – I did not come to destroy *the blueprint* (the Law and the Prophets), but I came to fulfill which really means – *to interpret the blueprint* so I can build Myself a Glorious House, comprised of Jews and Gentiles, grafted into My blueprint of Old (the Olive Tree, Romans 11) interpreted *anew*! (the New or the Renewed Covenant) So do not break *any* of the Commandments given through Moses. Rather keep them and teach them, and you will be *great*! But let *Me* Interpret them to you, not the Rabbis or all those who have burdened you with man-made laws and traditions that quench My Spirit...Rather let Me show you how to walk in Obedience to My Father. And then from verse 21 to 48 of Matthew 5, He proceeds to *reinterpret* the *blueprint* of *laws* and *commandments* to them...

"You have heard that it was said of old, 'YOU SHALL NOT MURDER,' and whoever murders will be in danger of the judgment. But I say to you that whoever is angry with his brother without a cause shall be in danger of the judgment..."

—Matthew 5:21, 22

"You have heard that it was said, 'YOU SHALL NOT COMMIT ADULTERY'; but I say to you that everyone who looks at a woman with lust for her has already committed adultery with her in his heart. If your right eye makes you stumble, tear it out and throw it from you; for it is better for you to lose one of the parts of your body, than for your whole body to be thrown into hell. If your right hand makes you stumble, cut it off and throw it from you; for it is better for you to lose one of the parts of your body, than for your whole body to go into hell."

—Matthew 5:27-30

"You have heard that it was said, 'AN EYE FOR AN EYE, AND A TOOTH FOR A TOOTH.' But I say to you, do not resist an evil person; but whoever slaps you on your right cheek, turn the other to him also. If anyone wants to sue you and take your shirt, let him have your coat also. Whoever forces you to go one mile, go with him two. Give to him who asks of you, and do not turn away from him who wants to borrow from you."

—Matthew 5:38-42

And on and on He goes reinterpreting the Torah, Laws, and Commandments to make them even more demanding. In order to truly obey them as He has charged us, we must have the Holy Spirit to help us and to change our hearts. This is the *mark* of the New or Renewed Covenant (Brit Chadasha in Hebrew) as written in the Book of Jeremiah,

"Behold, days are coming," declares Yahveh, "when I will make a new covenant with the house of Israel and with the house of Judah, not like the covenant which I made with their fathers in the day I took them by the hand to bring them out of the land of Egypt, My covenant which they broke, although I was a husband to them," declares Yahveh. "But this is the covenant which I will make with the house of Israel after those days," declares Yahveh, "I will put My law within them and on their heart I will write it; and I will be their God, and they shall be My people.

—Jeremiah 31:31-33

When both inwardly and outwardly we obey the Father's Commandments, we then walk in holiness.

"Pursue peace with all men and *Holiness* without which *no one* will see the LORD (Yeshua)"

—Hebrews 12:14

Many people are talking about "pursuing peace," being "peacemakers," and so were the Hippies in the '60s, but what about the *holiness*? In Hebrew – holiness is *Kdusha*, or Separateness.

It is about *separating* from all that is profane and all sin and pagan mixture.

Sin means to break the Father's Commandments.

"'therefore, COME OUT FROM THEIR MIDST AND BE SEPARATE,' says Yahveh. 'AND DO NOT TOUCH WHAT IS UNCLEAN; And I will welcome you. And I will be a father to you, And you shall be sons and daughters to Me,' Says Yahveh Almighty."

—2 Corinthians 6:17,18

It is also time to both repent and make restitution for the sins committed against the Jewish people in the name of Christ, both the sins of omission and commission. In 2 Samuel 21:1-3 it says,

Now there was a famine in the days of David for three years, year after year; and David sought the presence of Yahveh. And Yahveh said, "It is for Saul and his bloody house, because he put the Gibeonites to death." So the king called the Gibeonites and spoke to them (now the Gibeonites were not of the sons of Israel but of the remnant of the Amorites, and the sons of Israel made a covenant with them, but Saul had sought to kill them in his zeal for the sons of Israel and Judah). Thus David said to the Gibeonites, "What should I do for you? And how can I make atonement that you may bless the inheritance of Yahveh?"

—2 Samuel 21:1-3

Just like King David, the Gentile Christian church must make restitution for the sins committed against the Jewish people in past generations. We must bless Israel and the Jewish people *actively*, in prayer, and in practice! Then the drought will break, and the *rain* will come, and with it the Harvest!

And I will bless those who bless you, And the one who curses you I will curse. And in you all the families of the earth will be blessed."

—Genesis 12:3

Part Ten

Revocation of the Council of Nicaea

From the letter of the Emperor (Constantine) to all those not present at the council. (Found in Eusebius, Vita Const.,Lib III 18-20)

When the question relative to the sacred festival of Easter arose, it was universally thought that it would be convenient that all should keep the feast on one day; for what could be more beautiful and more desirable than to see this festival, through which we receive the hope of immortality, celebrated by all with one accord and in the same manner? It was declared to be particularly unworthy for this, the holiest of festivals, to follow the customs (the calculation) of the Jews who had soiled their hands with the most fearful of crimes, and whose minds were blinded. In rejecting their custom we may transmit to our descendants the legitimate mode of celebrating Easter; which we have observed from the time of the Saviour's passion (according to the day of the week).

We ought not, therefore, to have anything in common with the Jew, for the Saviour has shown us another way; our worship following a more legitimate and more convenient course (the order of the days of the week: And consequently in unanimously adopting this mode, we desire, dearest brethren to separate ourselves from the detestable company of the Jew. For it is truly shameful for us to hear them boast that without their direction, we could not keep this feast. How can they be in the right, they who, after the death of the Saviour, have no longer been led by reason but by wild violence, as their delusion may urge them? They do not possess the truth in this Easter question, for in their blindness and repugnance to all improvements they frequently celebrate two Passovers in the same year. We could not imitate those who are openly in error.

How, then, could we follow these Jews who are most certainly blinded by error? For to celebrate a Passover twice in one year, is totally inadmissible.

But even if this were not so it would still be your duty not to tarnish your soul by communication with such wicked people (the Jews). You should consider not only that the number of churches in these provinces make a majority, but also that it is right to demand what our reason approves, and that we should have nothing in common with the Jews. (Gleaned from Dr. Henry R. Percival's *"The Nicaean and Post Nicaean Fathers."* Vol. XIV Grand Rapid: Erdmans pub. 1979, pgs. 54-55)

Exposing the 23 Lies & Doctrinal Errors

1. "When the question relative to the sacred festival of Easter..."

The truth: sacred to pagan traditions, this is a pagan name derived from the goddess Ishtar. (Exodus 20:3, Hosea 2:17)

2. "...arose, it was universally..."

The truth: Everyone in the universe? Is Constantine the king of the universe? (Isaiah 14:3)

3. "...thought that it would be convenient..."

The truth: God does not call us to convenience but obedience. (John 15:10)

4. "...that all should keep the feast on one day; for what could be more beautiful and more desirable than to see this festival, through which we receive the hope of immortality, celebrated by all with one accord and in the same manner?...."

The truth: Without Jews? John 17:21, unity between Jew and Gentile brings the salvation of all mankind. (Psalms 133 and Isaiah 56)

5. "...It was declared to be particularly unworthy..."

The truth: Yahveh's choice of dates is "unworthy" to Constantine as he sets himself above God's choosing of timings. (Daniel 7:25 and Isaiah 14:13 [Lucifer])

6. "...for this, the holiest of festivals to follow the customs (the calculation) of the Jews..."

The truth: Which are the original and true calculations? (Leviticus 23:1, Jeremiah 31:31–34)

7. "...who had soiled their hands with the most fearful of crimes, and whose minds were blinded..."

The truth: In John 10:17–18 Yeshua lays His own life down (See also John 3:16.) the accusation that "The Jews killed Christ" has been the incentive for the extermination of millions of Jews from that point onwards and until this day, including the Holocaust. (See Matthew 7:17–20, the fruit of this theology)

8. "...In rejecting their custom..."

The truth: God's custom according to His Word.

9. "...we may transmit to our descendants the legitimate..."

The truth: according to Constantine but not according to the Word of God. (Matthew 26:2, Leviticus 23:1–4, Genesis 1:14, John 20:1–9, Matthew 12:39)

10. "...mode of celebrating Easter which we have observed..."

The truth: pagan name and feast not mentioned in the Holy Scriptures.

11. "We ought not therefore to have anything in common with the Jew, for the Savior has shown us another way"

The truth: Yeshua is Jewish, so if nothing is in common with the Jews, nothing is in common with the Messiah. (Matthew 1, John 19;19, Luke 1:59, Luke 2:21)

12. "our worship following a more legitimate and more convenient course, the order of the days of the week"

The truth: Constantine legitimizes his own ideas in order to gain political power and control and he attempts to dethrone the Word of God on this subject – setting himself and his opinions above Yah and His unchanging Word.

13. "...And consequently in unanimously..."

The truth: without the Jews from which salvation comes! (John 4:22)

14. "...adopting this mode, we desire, dearest brethren to separate ourselves from the detestable company of the Jew For it is truly shameful for us to hear them boast that without their direction we could not keep this feast. How can they be in the right, they who, after the death of the Savior..."

The truth: Romans 11:15–20 warns the Gentiles not to be arrogant against the Jews or Gentiles will be cut of the Olive tree!

15. "...have no longer been led by reason..."

The truth: True sons of God are not led by reason or Greek philosophy but by the Spirit of God. Since Constantine and the Council of Nicaea, the church in its vast majority has been led by reason and by theologians instead of by powerful apostles. (Romans 8:14, Ephesians 2:20) – these are all Jewish.

16. "but by wild violence, as their delusion may urge them"

The truth: What wild violence is he talking about? Unsupported accusation used many times to incite the masses against the Jews like in the Protocols of the Elders of Zion?

17. "They do not possess the truth in this Easter question, for in their blindness and [15th lie] repugnance to all improvements"

The truth: traditions of demons and men that make null and void the Word of God (Matthew 15:3,4, Mark 7:13)

18. "They frequently celebrate two Passovers in the same year. We could not imitate those who are openly in error. How, then, could we follow these Jews who are most certainly blinded by error?"

The truth: Is following the biblical customs error? Who is really blinded here? Gentiles are supposed to be grafted into Israel's Olive tree and not vice versa! (Romans 11:15–20)

19. "For to celebrate a Passover twice in one year is totally inadmissible."

The truth: 2 Chronicles 30:1–3, it is totally scriptural.

20. "But even if this were not so it would still be your duty not to tarnish your soul by communication with such wicked people (the Jews)."

The truth: In other words, Constantine's purpose is to separate from the Jews and the Torah no matter what! Why? 1 John 4:1–3 states that the spirit of anti-Messiah, in operation through Constantine, removes the identity of Messiah as a Jew, and sets himself above God and His Word and His sovereign choice of choosing the Jews to bring salvation.

21. "You should consider not only that the number of churches in these provinces make a majority"

The truth: God has never worked with "majorities" but with obedience. Trusting in the arm of the flesh or the opinions of men brings about a curse! (Deuteronomy 28:1–14, Jeremiah 17:5, Judges 7:2–8,1 Samuel 14:6)

22. "...but also that it is right to demand what our reason approves..."

The truth: Human reasoning? (1 Corinthians 1:27, Isaiah 29:14b)

23. "...and that we should have nothing in common with the Jews."

The truth: or with the Jewish Messiah or His salvation – John 4:22, Romans 11:15–20. He set the Gentile part of the church onto a path of self-destruction, remaining a wild olive instead of being grafted into the cultivated Olive tree – which is Israel – because of arrogance, removing the foundations of the Jewish apostles and prophets. (Psalms 11:3, Ephesians 2:20, Revelation 21:14)

Prayer Renouncing the First Council of Nicaea

Please pray. You can copy and pass it on, and please let us know of your decision.

Before the Almighty God of Israel, I stand and hereby renounce the First Council of Nicaea as led by Constantine. I renounce its foundation and all the anti-Jewish fruit that came out of it. I renounce every doctrinal error and every lie in it, including replacement theology in all of its aspects.

I hereby affirm my faith in Yahveh, the God of Israel, who is the Creator of the Universe and my Father through the atoning death of His Holy Son Yeshua, who is both the promised Jewish Messiah and God in the flesh. I hereby affirm my faith in the resurrection of Yeshua the Messiah and the outpouring of the Holy Spirit of God from the Day of Shavuot (Pentecost) and onwards, to all that repent and believe in the Son. I hereby affirm my belief that I am grafted into the Olive Tree that represents Israel, and together with the believing Jewish people, I will inherit eternal life. I hereby affirm that the God of Israel will never forsake His people, neither will He forget His covenant with the Jews or with the Ecclesia (Called out Ones - Church).

I thank you, Holy Father, for removing all the curses that have come into my life and into my nation due to our belief in the tenets of faith stated in the Council of Nicaea concerning the Jews and the Jewish foundations of the faith. I beg you and thank you for pouring out your great mercy and forgiveness over myself, my family, and my nation. I hereby commit myself to walk in truth as You reveal it to me and in love with all my fellow men and especially my (and the Church's) spiritual parents, the Jewish people, according to Genesis 12:1-3.

End Word

Closure

THE PURPOSE OF THIS booklet is to expose and to stir you up to be part of this heavenly MAP Revolution. This is not a theological book but rather a *prophetic call* to rebel against the wicked anti-Messiah principality that has been ruling the theology and lifestyle of most Christians to this day. This is a spiritual battle, and it needs to be fought with Spiritual Weapons! Remember,

Love, forgiveness, truth, integrity, holiness, prayer, and *obedience* are lethal weapons against the Kingdom of Darkness

And now come back with me to the 21st century, the era of Media and Communication with such high technology that cloning humans has been made possible but stopping storms and hurricanes *not*. To the 21st century, where gay parades, called "Pride Parades" (and rightly so!) are the norm in America and Europe and are threatening even the Holy City of Jerusalem. This century of so many conflicts all over the world and especially the Palestinian Uprising that has threatened the very existence of the tiny nation of Israel with reviving Islam and anti-Jewish attitudes in Europe and other places. This is a century of contrasts, conflicts, battles, expectations, gross immorality, rampant abortion, and sexual promiscuity... Borderline Sodom and Gomorrah? The situation is so deadly in the USA and all over the world with the earthquakes, tsunamis, and devastating hurricanes increasing by the hour... the stage is set for a World Solution, but prior to the revealing of the Anti-Christ, by the One World Order, the Almighty has prepared a *Holy Banquet*. There will be an amazing outpouring of His Grace and a Revival of breathtaking signs, wonders, miracles, and Angelic Visitations, a harvest of such magnitude that the world has *never* seen! Only those who are willing to repent and be sanctified from deadly Anti-Christ* theologies and be purified by His truth and Holy Fire will enjoy it and lead it.

"Sanctify them in the truth; Your word is truth."

—John 17:17

---

* These are theologies that are anti Messsiah, His Word, His Jewish people and His Holy Spirit. These theologies cause the Body to be sick with sin, iniquity, immorality and hatred and thus causes the Anointing of the Holy Spirit to leave. Yeshua said that the *key* for *unity* which is the key for *revival* is to be sanctified by His Truth. "Sanctify them by the truth, Your word is truth...That they may be one...That the world will know that you sent Me." – John 17:17-21

The unity between Jews and Gentiles in Messiah following this sanctification will bring forth the long-awaited End time Revival.

That they may all be one; even as You, Father, are in Me and I in You, that they also may be in Us, so that the world may believe that You sent Me.

—John 17:21

Appendix

Connect With Us

Other Books

Order now online: www.kad-esh.org/shop/

Defeating Depression
Find Out Why Revival Does Not Come... Yet!

The Identity Theft
The Return of the 1st Century Messiah

From Sickology to a Healthy Logic
The Product of 18 Years Walking Through Psychiatric
Hospitals

ATG: Addicts Turning to God
The Biblical Way to Handle Addicts and Addictions

The Healing Power of the Roots
It's a Matter of Life or Death!

Grafted In
It's Time to Take the Nation's!

Sheep Nations
It's Time to Take the Nations!

Restoring the Glory: The Original Way
The Ancient Paths Rediscovered

Stormy Weather
Judgment Has Already Begun, Revival is Knocking at the
Door

Yeshua is the Name
The Important Restoration of the Original
Hebrew Name of the Messiah

The Bible Cure for Africa and the Nations
The Key to the Restoration of All Africa

The Key of Abraham
The Blessing or the Curse?

Yes!
The Dramatic Salvation of
Archbishop Dr. Dominiquae Bierman

Eradicating the Cancer of Religion
Hint: All People Have It

Restoration of Holy Giving
Releasing the True 1,000 Fold Blessing

Vision Negev
The Awesome Restoration of the Sephardic Jews

The Woman Factor by Rabbi Baruch Bierman
Freedom From Womanphobia

The Revival of the Third Day (Free E-Book)
The Return to Yeshua the Jewish Messiah

Music Albums
www.kad-esh.org/shop/
The Key of Abraham
Abba Shebashamayim
Uru
Retorno

Get Equipped & Partner with Us

Global Revival MAP (GRM) Israeli Bible School
Take the most comprehensive video Bible school online that
focuses on dismantling replacement theology.
For more information or to order, please contact us:

www.grmbibleschool.com
grm@dominiquaebierman.com

United Nations for Israel Movement

We invite you to join us as a member and partner with $25 a month, which supports the advancing of this End time vision that will bring true unity to the body of the Messiah. We will see the One New Man form, witness the restoration of Israel, and take part in the birthing of SHEEP NATIONS. Today is an exciting time to be serving Him!

www.unitednationsforisrael.org

info@unitednationsforisrael.org

Global Re-Education Initiative (GRI)
Against Anti-Semitism

Discover the Jewishness of the Messiah and defeat Christian anti-Semitism with this online video course to see revival in your nation!

www.against-antisemitism.com

info@against-antisemitism.com

Join Our Annual Israel Tours

Travel through the Holy Land and watch the Hebrew Holy Scriptures come alive.

www.kad-esh.org/tours-and-events/

To Send Offerings to Support our Work

Your help keeps this mission of restoration going far and wide.

www.kad-esh.org/donations

CONTACT US

Archbishop Dr. Dominiquae & Rabbi Baruch Bierman

Kad-Esh MAP Ministries | www.kad-esh.org
info@kad-esh.org

United Nations for Israel | www.unitednationsforisrael.org
info@unitednationsforisrael.org

Zion's Gospel Press | shalom@zionsgospel.com
52 Tuscan Way, Ste 202-412, 32092 St. Augustine Florida,
USA
+1-972-301-7087

CPSIA information can be obtained
at www.ICGtesting.com
Printed in the USA
LVHW022109290821
696385LV00007B/1286